Steve Yzerman was the league's third highest scorer in 1989.

RED WINGS
DETROIT

BY ROSS RENNIE

CREATIVE EDUCATION INC.

Published by Creative Education, Inc.
123 S. Broad Street, Mankato, Minnesota 56001

Designed by Rita Marshall
Photos by Bruce Bennett Studios,
Frank Howard/Protography and Wide World Photos

Copyright © 1990 Creative Education, Inc.
International copyrights reserved in all countries.
No part of this book may be reproduced in any form
without written permission from the publisher.
Printed in the United States of America

Library of Congress Cataloging-in-Publication Data

Rennie, Ross.
  The Detroit Red Wings/by Ross Rennie.
    p.   cm.
  Summary: Presents, in text and illustrations, the history of
the Detroit Red Wings hockey team.
    ISBN 0-88682-277-7
    1. Detroit Red Wings (Hockey team)—History—Juvenile literature.
[1. Detroit Red Wings (Hockey team)—History.   2. Hockey—History.]
I. Title.
GV848.D47R46   1989
796.96′264′0977434—dc20   89-37732
                                                              CIP
                                                              AC

THE BEGINNINGS: 1926–1938

Detroit is home to the American automobile industry. In the United States, Detroit and cars are one in the same thing. This city is also the subject of an unusual trivia question that asks, "What is the first foreign country you hit if you head south from Detroit?" Many folks are surprised that the answer is Canada. It is because of this closeness to Canada that there is a long history of hockey in Detroit. In fact, because of the prosperity brought about by the auto industry, Detroit has grown into the fifth-

1 9 2 6

The Red Wings played their first NHL game November 18 against the Boston Bruins. Detroit lost 2–0.

largest U.S. city. As such, the area has been able to support professional teams in virtually every sport, including football, baseball, basketball, and, of course, hockey.

The city built on cars has had a team in the National Hockey League since 1926. The original club was established when a Detroit syndicate purchased the Victoria Cougars hockey team for a mere hundred thousand dollars. Three of the original members of the team, Frank Frederickson, Frank Foyston, and Jack Walker, were eventually to become members of the Hockey Hall of Fame.

By the end of the team's first season, they had lost a lot of money and desperately needed someone to manage the team. It was then, in 1927, that Jack Adams would begin his long and successful association with the team. Before the association was finished, Jack Adams and the Detroit Red Wings would become synonymous.

It was not until the 1932–33 season that the team started to come together. Perhaps part of the reason for the change in the team that year was their new name. A noted American industry leader, James Norris, had bought the Detroit franchise in 1932. Norris had played hockey in Canada years before in Montreal on a team called the Winged Wheelers. He used that "winged wheel" as the insignia for his newly acquired team. It seemed to him a natural choice for a club from the motor city. The team's name was also changed to reflect the new insignia. The team remains the Detroit Red Wings to this day.

Norris added some respectability to the team, while Jack Adams added some talent and, for a change, had the opportunity to really coach the team. The reversal was quick.

By 1934, the Red Wings were a powerhouse. They had little trouble beating the Toronto Maple Leafs that year in

Jack Adams would be proud of Detroit's current personnel, including the talented Rick Zombo.

1 9 3 6

With the talent gathered by James Norris and Jack Adams, Detroit won their first Stanley Cup.

the Stanley Cup semifinal. It was on to the finals for the first time in the club's history. Detroit's adversary was the Chicago Blackhawks, and Chicago prevailed that year in a close contest. Norris was unhappy at the result and went on a spending spree to obtain the talent needed to win the Cup.

Over the next couple of years, Adams acquired players such as Bucko McDonald from Buffalo, Hec Kilrea from Toronto, and Syd Howe and Scotty Bowman from St. Louis. To obtain Howe and Bowman, Norris paid more than fifty thousand dollars a player. For those days, that was an enormous sum of money, especially considering it was in the middle of the Great Depression. Needless to say, Norris wanted to win a Stanley Cup very badly.

Despite all his efforts, the rebuilt team scored a lot of goals but did not even make the 1935 play-offs. Yet the money and effort were not wasted—not if you followed the team into the 1935–36 season. With the talent acquired over the past years and the opportunity to practice together as a team, the Red Wings once again finished in first place in the American Division. This time the play-offs would be far more rewarding. For the first time in the team's history, their names appeared on the Stanley Cup. Together, James Norris and Jack Adams had made their mark on the hockey world. Their efforts and dedication to the sport would, forty years later, lead to both their names being used to identify two of the four NHL modern-day divisions, a high compliment indeed!

It was not only the great scorers who contributed to Detroit's success, but also the goaltending of Norm Smith. Smith registered six shutouts in both the 1936 and 1937 seasons. The latter led the way to yet another first-place finish and a second Stanley Cup victory. This time around things were a lot tougher. The first round of play-offs was against the Montreal Canadiens. The five-game series was a physical contest. Detroit survived, but just barely. When the final series began against the New York Rangers, injuries had reduced the roster to just nine players. Norm Smith, also injured, had to be replaced by borrowed goaltender Earl Robertson. Robertson was a goalie for the Rangers' rival team, the New York Americans. With a lot of patchwork and home-ice advantage, Detroit managed to win the final game and the Cup. They had now won two NHL championships in a row. Talk of a Detroit dynasty was heard throughout the league.

Detroit began rebuilding and continued to add quality players, like Marcel Pronovost, throughout its history.

Adams believed he had a winning team and decided not to make any roster changes for the 1937–38 season. That was to prove to be a mistake. The club finished in fourth place, winning only twelve games and matching their worst-ever record. In true Adams fashion, he admitted it was his fault. He stated, "After this flop, I'll never hesitate to bust up championship clubs." He may have been the first coach to admit that particular mistake, but he certainly was not the last coach to make the same error.

THE WAR YEARS: 1939–1949

The NHL was restructured during this period. Instead of two separate Canadian and American divisions, all of the teams were in a single division. The Red Wings started rebuilding the team with trades. In 1938 alone, they completed trades with four other teams. When World War II started, it became difficult to assemble the quality of talent they needed to complete the effort. By 1942 an

As in the 1940s, Detroit rebuilt during the '80s with talent such as Adam Oates. (pages 10–11)

Although Gordie Howe would not join the Red Wings until 1946, Detroit won its third Stanley Cup.

almost new Detroit Red Wings team managed a fifth-place finish, good enough to qualify for postseason play.

Although the Detroit team had not excelled during the regular season, they peaked at the right time, advancing to the championship series against the Toronto Maple Leafs.

Detroit won the first three games of the final series. It appeared as if a sweep was in the making. The Red Wings were ahead 3–2 in the fourth game with only minutes left in the third period. The champagne was being cooled for the victory celebration. Referee Mel Harwood then assessed penalties to the Red Wings that resulted in two Toronto goals, and a Maple Leaf victory. At the end of the game, three Red Wings surrounded Harwood, and Jack Adams slid across the ice to join the heated discussion. The accounts of what happened next vary greatly depending on the source of the account. The result is recorded in NHL history. Adams was suspended for the remainder of the series for apparently hitting the referee.

The Toronto Maple Leafs went on to write a unique chapter in NHL history as the only team in the NHL Stanley Cup finals to lose the first three games and then eventually win the Cup. Detroit felt robbed. They could never undo the defeat of 1942. But it took only one season to regain at least some of their pride. Frank Calder, who most Detroit fans blamed for the reversal in 1942, never lived to see the Red Wings demolish the Boston Bruins in four straight games to win the 1943 Stanley Cup. Sid Abel led the team that year and, as the team captain, he made sure the same fate would not befall the team two years in a row.

Ted Lindsay, future member of the "Production Line," joined the Red Wings.

As the war ended, a number of hockey stars returned to the NHL. That made it difficult for any team to maintain a position of strength. Toronto and Montreal traded Stanley Cups while the other four NHL teams, including Detroit, were out of championship contention. A new era began on October 16, 1946, when a new Detroit Red Wing scored his first NHL goal against sturdy Turk Broda of the Toronto Maple Leafs. That young fellow, Gordie Howe, would eventually score hundreds more in a Detroit jersey and become a legend in NHL history. In 1947 Dit Clapper of the Boston Bruins had retired from hockey after twenty years in the NHL. At the time, this set a longevity record for the league. Howe would eclipse that record and many more before he finally hung up his skates.

It was Jack Adams who said "hockey has its superstars but it has only one superman, and that's Gordie Howe." Howe's career would span five decades, and before his retirement at the incredible age of fifty-one, Gordie would rewrite the NHL record books.

1 9 4 9

The Red Wings won their first of seven consecutive regular season titles.

Sid Abel, Ted Lindsay, and Gordie Howe would eventually combine on what became known as "the Production Line." It was aptly named for the automobile production workers in Detroit, and for the unbelievable goal-scoring ability the three players possessed. Together they forged the scoring strength that led to the strong comeback of the Red Wing teams of the 1950s.

As the 1940s drew to a close, Detroit began their streak of first-place finishes in the NHL. Under new coach Tommy Ivan, who took over the reins from Jack Adams in 1947, the Red Wings' franchise would have its most successful period ever. The Detroit team featured such players as Terry Sawchuck in goal, Lindsay, Howe, and Abel on offense, and Red Kelly and Marcel Pronovost on defense.

THE PRODUCTION YEARS: 1950–1959

The 1950s began like the 1940s had ended, with their second straight first-place finish. It would prove to be the second in a string of seven consecutive seasons in the top spot. The Red Wings would convert this success into Stanley Cup victories in 1950, 1952, 1954, and 1955.

The 1950 play-offs were probably the most notable for Detroit. Both series went the full seven games. Perhaps you could say the final series went beyond seven games, since it needed overtime for a decision.

In the semifinals against Toronto, Gordie Howe suffered a concussion that nearly ended his life. When he was rushed to the hospital, Gordie, in typical Howe fashion,

Like the incredible Gordie Howe, John Ogrodnick was a prolific scorer during the 1980s.

mumbled to Jack Adams, "Sorry I couldn't help more tonight." Howe's medical condition was serious enough that his mother flew from Saskatchewan to be by his side for what was considered by most to be his final hours. The sometimes-brutal punishment Gordie Howe inflicted on many of his opponents in the years that followed was testimony to his survival as well as his intention never again to be taken advantage of by another player.

Perhaps it was the serious injury to Howe in the series against Toronto that sparked his teammates to victory. Regardless of the reason, the Red Wings moved into the Stanley Cup final round against the New York Rangers. Jack Adams felt this matchup brought out the best in his

Alex Delvecchio was a vital part of the Red Wings success in the 1950s. (pages 18–19)

Terry Sawchuck was flawless in goal during the play-offs.

team. "That series," he said, "gave my kind of player the chance to shine." And shine they did! Despite the injury to Howe, the Red Wings prevailed and defeated New York in the seventh and deciding game in overtime to put an end to the Rangers' hopes and raise the fourth Stanley Cup banner to the rafters of the Detroit rink.

In both 1951 and 1952, the team was able to accomplish what no other Detroit team has been able to match since. Both years they accumulated one hundred or more points in the regular season. The feat is even more remarkable when it is considered that the season consisted of seventy games at that time. Today, even with an eighty-game schedule, few teams are able to amass one hundred or more points in the regular season.

The team was so strong in those days that they tried to set up challenges to keep the team producing. Howe was hitting his stride, and as the 1952 season drew to a close, he had his sights on tying Rocket Richard's fifty-goal record. Jack Adams wanted Howe to reach or break the record. He ordered Ivan, the coach, to play Gordie as often as possible in the last few games. However, it seemed that every time Howe got the puck he passed it to Sid Abel. Finally, in frustration, Tommy Ivan asked Howe what he was doing. It turned out Howe was trying to help Abel reach the twenty-goal mark, for which Abel would receive a bonus. Despite Howe's help, Abel ended the season with seventeen goals; Howe had scored forty-seven, three shy of the record.

The Red Wings captured the Stanley Cup behind the invincible play of Gordie Howe.

The 1952 season helped to heal the wounds of the great reversal of 1942. It was called, appropriately, "the Great Sweep." No team in NHL history had previously won both the semifinals and final play-off series without a single defeat. Detroit started the sweep with four wins over the Toronto Maple Leafs. In the finals, they met the mighty Montreal Canadiens, a team that boasted a strong defense and Rocket Richard's scoring power. Injuries hampered Montreal, and they also were beaten in four straight games by the Red Wings. The stingy Detroit goalie that year, Terry Sawchuk, gave up only five goals in the eight games played in the two series. That still stands as a play-off record for the Wings.

When teams are as strong as the Red Wings of the early 1950s were, tough defenseman like Red Kelly can be nice guys. Three times during the 1950s Kelly won the Lady Byng Trophy, which is given to the player combining a high standard of playing ability and gentlemanly conduct. It was in 1953 that All-Star Al Arbour joined the Detroit Red Wings. He was a league-leading defenseman, but it

was something else that made Al stand out from the rest of the players: he wore eyeglasses. He certainly did not let them get in his way of being a successful defenseman and eventually a Stanley Cup-winning coach with the New York Islanders.

The Boston Bruins dashed Detroit's play-off hopes in 1953, but the next two seasons the Red Wings easily defeated the Toronto Maple Leafs in semifinal action and then beat the Montreal Canadiens in a tough seven-game final series. These sixth and seventh Stanley Cup victories would have to sustain fan support for the team for many years to come. They were to be the last for over thirty-five years.

As the fifties came to a close, the Detroit boom turned to bust. In 1959 Detroit fell to sixth and last spot in the NHL regular-season standings. The team that had spent the first half of the decade in first place was now out of the play-offs for the first time in over twenty years. Things would get better, but not without some tough decisions.

1 9 5 5

A model of consistency, Alex Delvecchio helped the Red Wings capture another Stanley Cup victory.

LOTS OF CHANGES: 1960–1979

With a lot of players coming and going, Detroit managed to grab the last play-off spot in both 1960 and 1961. In 1960 they were defeated by Toronto, but in 1961 they made it once again to the finals. This time they faced the Chicago Blackhawks. In goal were Terry Sawchuk for the Wings and Glenn Hall for Chicago. Hall, who had been traded to Chicago in 1957 along with Ted Lindsay, came back to haunt his old team. The Blackhawks were on their way to winning their third Stanley Cup, and Detroit was not strong enough to stop them.

Despite Marcel Dionne's talent, the Red Wings of the 1970s were as unsuccessful as the 1959 team.

Goalie Terry Sawchuck was selected to the NHL All-Star team for the seventh time.

Terry Sawchuk played with Detroit during most of the 1950s and 1960s. Sawchuk set many team and NHL records in those two decades. He holds the NHL record for the most career games by a goaltender (971) and most career shutouts (103). In addition, the Detroit team records held by Terry Sawchuk include most games played (734), most wins (352), most shutouts (85), most seasons (10), most play-off wins (47), and most play-off shutouts (11).

When the team missed the play-offs in 1962, Bruce Norris, who owned the team, decided major changes were needed. The biggest change was the departure of Jack Adams's. After thirty-six years, it was time for some new blood in the front office. Adams was very upset over the news. No matter how nice Norris tried to be, Adams stated bluntly, "I was kicked out." With Adams gone, a new era began. During his tenure in the league, Adams had his

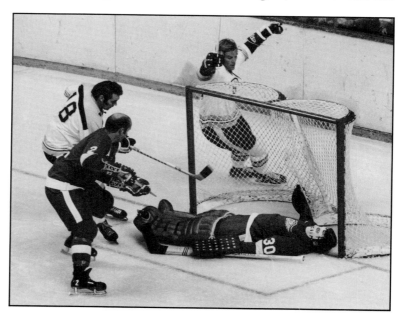

Goaltender Roy Edwards won over ninety games for Detroit during the 1960s and '70s.

name engraved on Lord Stanley's Cup as a player, coach, and general manager. He is the only person in NHL history to be represented on the Cup in all three capacities.

Sid Abel was now the general manager as well as coach. Trades were the order of the day. More trades occurred in Detroit in the 1960s and 1970s than had been made in the team's history to that point. Doug Barkley came to Detroit in a trade with Chicago in 1962. He helped the team reach the Stanley Cup finals in 1963, 1964, and 1966. Unfortunately for Doug and the Red Wings, an accidental blow blinded him in one eye and ended his hockey career in 1966. Some hockey analysts believe the loss of Barkley started the decline of the Detroit Red Wing fortunes over the next twenty years. The truth is more likely a combination of many factors, including NHL expansion, rapid coaching changes, and the loss of Gordie Howe first to retirement and then to a rival league.

Gordie Howe ended his career in Detroit, leaving behind a host of NHL records.

Gordie Howe had started in Detroit in 1946. He insisted on a Detroit Red Wings jacket as a signing bonus. One of his most prized possessions was a watch earned by scoring a big goal for his Wings. For all of that, Detroit received twenty-five years of loyal service, including 1,687 games, 786 goals, 1,023 assists, 158 play-off points, and four Stanley Cups. Not a bad investment. For his efforts, Gordie Howe collected six Hart Trophies as the league's leading scorer, twenty-one All-Star game selections, and more NHL records than you can count. He owns or shares more NHL records than any other player. Howe truly earned his nickname, "Mr. Hockey."

In 1971 Howe retired from playing hockey with Detroit, moving to the front office. His absence from the bench left a big gap to fill. After all, who could fill superman's shoes?

Steve Yzerman's splendid play in the 1980s was reminiscent of the legendary Gordie Howe. (pages 26–27)

Howe, to everyone's surprise, did not stay retired very long. The Houston Aeros of the World Hockey Association made Gordie an offer too tempting to refuse. They enabled his dream to come true—to play professional hockey alongside his sons Marty and Mark. Gordie left a void in both Detroit and the NHL. To some, "the King" had not only abdicated, but had become a traitor.

In 1973 Alex Delvecchio moved from player to coach. He coached the team for three years. The Red Wings had missed qualifying for the play-offs in the previous three years, and in six of the last seven. When Delvecchio took the helm, things did not improve. The team missed postseason play each year Alex coached them. The Red Wings knew improvement was needed.

Changes became the norm for the Red Wings. From 1974 to 1979, Detroit had no less than fifteen team captains. During the same period, there were six different coaches. It is no wonder that Detroit missed the play-offs every year but one.

TODAY'S DETROIT RED WINGS:
THE 1980S AND BEYOND

As the team entered the 1980s, the revolving door into and out of the coach's office continued to spin faster and faster. Ten people filled the position during the decade. None were better than Jacques Demers, who started in the spot in 1986. He brought a sense of discipline, pride, and permanence that had been missing from the position for many years.

In the first year, Demers was responsible for bringing some needed control to his club. The results were dramatic. Detroit doubled their wins over the prior year and finished second in the Norris Division, just one point behind the division-leading St. Louis Blues. In the play-offs, the team won the division championship for the first time in club history. In the Campbell Conference championship round, they lost to the Stanley Cup champions that year, the Edmonton Oilers. For his efforts, Jack Demers won the Jack Adams Award as coach of the year, the first Detroit coach ever to win the award.

With players like Steve Yzerman, Detroit's first draft choice in 1983, the team looked to a bright future. Yzerman, at age twenty-one, became the youngest team captain in Red Wing history. When he appeared, at age eighteen, in the 1984 NHL All-Star game, he set an NHL record as the youngest player ever to appear in that contest. Many folks believe that with more mature wingers, Yzerman could be

1 9 8 6

Joe Kocur was another young talent that Jacques Demers added to his club.

29

Glen Hanlon proved to be a consistent performer for Detroit in the 1980s.

Forward Gerard Gallant was named to the All-Star team in 1989.

31

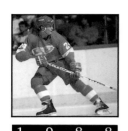

Bob Probert smoothly meshed his fine offensive talents with aggressive play.

as prolific a scorer as Mario Lemieux or Wayne Gretzky.

There were a lot of other exciting forwards on the Detroit team, such as Gerard Gallant, Petr Klima, Paul Mac-Lean, and Adam Oates. With a mixture of youth and experience, the Red Wings have the potential to produce championship teams. The goaltending duo of Glen Hanlon and Greg Stefan should provide the strength and backup needed in that critical position. Detroit also had some solid defensemen including Mike O'Connell, Lee Norwood, Doug Halward, and Gilbert Delmore.

Jack Demers continued his winning ways as coach in the 1987–88 season, when the team finished first in the Norris Division. The last time the team had finished at the top of their division was in 1965, twenty-three years earlier. At the end of the season, Demers was rewarded by becoming the NHL's first coach ever to win the Jack Adams Trophy twice. The hard work of the players had quickly moved the worst team in the NHL toward becoming one of the league's elite teams once again.

It will not be long before many new, exciting, and successful chapters will be added to the history of this remarkable team from the Motor City. Detroit Red Wing fans have been treated to the thrills provided by numerous Hockey Hall of Famers of the past. Undoubtably, future members of that institution will play on Detroit teams, and the thrills they will provide will be no less exciting than those of the giants of the past.